25538330

1/07

WE THE PEOPLE

Women of the Harlem Renaissance

by Lisa Beringer McKissack

Content Adviser: Marcellus Blount, Ph.D.,
Associate Professor, Department of English and Comparative Literature,
Columbia University

Reading Adviser: Rosemary G. Palmer, Ph.D.,
Department of Literacy, College of Education,
Boise State University

Compass Point Books ◆ Minneapolis, Minnesota

Compass Point Books
3109 West 50th Street, #115
Minneapolis, MN 55410

Visit Compass Point Books on the Internet at *www.compasspointbooks.com*
or e-mail your request to *custserv@compasspointbooks.com*

On the cover: *Harlem: Art Class,* c.1939–1940. Oil on plywood by William H. Johnson

Photographs ©: Smithsonian American Art Museum, Washington, D.C./Art Resource N.Y., cover; Prints Old and Rare, back cover (far left); Library of Congress, back cover; Bettman/Corbis, 5, 16, 27; Underwood & Underwood/Corbis, 7, 40; Yale Collection of American Literature, Beinecke Rare Book and Manuscript Library, 8, 12; Library of Congress, 9, 10, 20, 21, 22, 24, 37; Corbis, 15; Photographs and Prints Division, Schomburg Center for Research in Black Culture, The New York Public Library, Astor, Lenox and Tilden Foundations, 17, 19, 32; General Research Division, The New York Public Library, Astor, Lenox and Tilden Foundations, 25; Time Life Pictures/Getty Images, 29; Smithsonian American Art Museum, Washington D.C./Art Resource, N.Y., 30; Painting of Bessie Smith courtesy of "The Jazz Masters Series by BRUNI" BRUNI Gallery, 33; Frank Diggs Collection/Getty Images, 34, 36; 2006 The Jacob and Gwendolyn Lawrence Foundation, Seattle/Artists Rights Society (ARS), New York/Art Resources, N.Y., 39.

Editor: Julie Gassman
Page Production: Bobbie Nuytten
Photo Researcher: Lori Bye
Cartographer: XNR Productions, Inc.
Library Consultant: Kathleen Baxter

Art Director: Jaime Martens
Creative Director: Keith Griffin
Editorial Director: Carol Jones
Managing Editor: Catherine Neitge

Library of Congress Cataloging-in-Publication Data
McKissack, Lisa Beringer.
  Women of the Harlem Renaissance / by Lisa Beringer McKissack.
     p. cm.— (We the people)
  Includes bibliographical references and index.
  Audience: Grades 4–6.
  ISBN-13: 978-0-7565-2034-2 (library binding)
  ISBN-10: 0-7565-2034-7 (library binding)
  ISBN-13: 978-0-7565-2046-5 (paperback)
  ISBN-10: 0-7565-2046-0 (paperback)
 1. Harlem Renaissance—Juvenile literature. 2. African American women—Biography—Juvenile
literature. 3. African American women authors—Biography—Juvenile literature. 4. African American women
artists—Biography—Juvenile literature. 5. African American women singers—Biography—Juvenile literature.
6. African Americans—New York (State)—New York—Intellectual life—20th century—Juvenile literature. 7.
African American arts—New York (State)—New York—20th century—Juvenile literature. 8. Harlem (New York,
N.Y.)—Biography—Juvenile literature. 9. New York (N.Y.)—Biography—Juvenile literature. I. Title. II. Series.
  E185.6.M48 2007
  305.48'896073074710922—dc22 [B]   2006027095

TABLE OF CONTENTS

A RENAISSANCE BEGINS

The smooth sound of an alto sax could be heard floating in the air on a hot summer night. People gathered to hear poets read their latest works, while others rushed to the nearest gallery to see a new sculpture being unveiled. This was Harlem in its renaissance.

A renaissance occurs when people begin express-ing ideas in new and exciting ways. The New York City community of Harlem experienced a cultural renaissance during the 1920s and 1930s. African-American leaders in arts and literature settled in the community to support and inspire one another, and soon word spread. People from all over the country relocated there to study, work, and play. At night, Harlem was the place to be and to be seen. Cool jazz. Good conversation. New ideas and creativity. All of this was Harlem. And everybody wanted to be a part of it.

There were other all-black neighborhoods in New York and in other large cities, but none equaled Harlem.

Harlem nightclubs were filled with the energy of people dancing, talking, and laughing together.

Harlem was special. It represented opportunity, freedom of expression, and hope. One historian described Harlem as "the biggest and most elegant black community in the Western world." And for black women, this era represented the dawn of a new day, one filled with promise and possibility.

At the time, both black and white women in the United States were expected to stay home and care for their families. No woman, regardless of her race, was allowed to vote until 1920. But African-American women were more disadvantaged than white women. Black women had

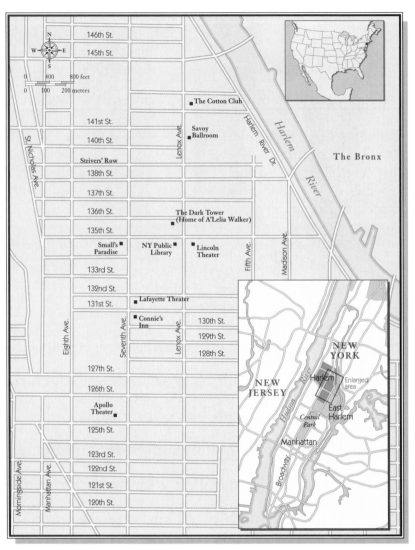

Harlem is a 2-square mile (5.2-square kilometer) neighborhood in Manhattan.

a harder time getting into college or finding a job that didn't

involve physical work such as doing laundry, waiting tables, or

being a nanny. But Harlem gave black women opportunities

to express themselves, and people began to listen.

Women came from all over the country. A young nurse from Chicago pursued her dream of writing. Another from Philadelphia became a powerful editor. A vibrant and curious writer from Florida found an audience for her stories of the rural South. A young, talented sculptor became one of the leading artists of her day. And a young musician rose from the vaudeville stage to become one of the greatest singers in history. These women were not just inspired by the Harlem Renaissance. They became the Harlem Renaissance.

Well-dressed women and girls walked down Lexington Avenue in the heart of Harlem.

NELLA LARSEN: FROM NURSE TO NOVELIST

Nella Larsen (1891–1964) was born in Chicago to a white dressmaker from Denmark and a black man from the Danish West Indies. One historian believes that her father may have been a light-skinned black man who passed for white—an action that was risky because people of both races often viewed it as a betrayal. Getting caught could lead to serious trouble. If white people found out, they might try to kill him. Blacks often excluded those who chose to "pass." Despite the risk, some African Americans passed in order to

Author Nella Larsen

gain greater opportunities that were normally extended only to white people.

No one knows for sure, but some historians believe Larsen's family may have disowned her because she was too dark-skinned to pass. In 1907, her parents sent her to Fisk University Normal School in Nashville, Tennessee. Larsen left Fisk before the end of the school year, following a visit

Since Fisk University was established in 1866, it has educated many black leaders, including Thurgood Marshall, the first African-American Supreme Court justice.

from her mother. No one knows what was discussed, but she never saw her parents again.

She eventually made her way to New York City where, in 1912, she started nursing school at the Lincoln Hospital and Home. She graduated three years later and settled in Harlem.

It was an exciting place to be! There were bands to hear, theater to attend, and interesting people to meet. One such person was a physicist named Elmer Imes. Nella and Elmer married in 1919.

The two became friends with the most important writers, thinkers, and social activists in Harlem and were considered part of the "Talented Tenth." This was the name W.E.B. DuBois gave to a small group of well-educated blacks. An outstanding educator and writer, DuBois was one of the most important political leaders of his generation. Inspired by her new friends, Larsen became a writer.

She wrote two novels, which were published, and many short stories and articles. Her writing mirrored her life as a biracial woman. Color bias was common among African-Americans at that time. Sometimes fair-skinned blacks were treated with more respect by other blacks and whites, and sometimes they were mistreated because they "weren't black enough." Some blacks defined people

W.E.B. DuBois (1868–1963)

by skin color in the same way whites did, so the lighter you were, the better you may have been treated. Larsen used her writing as a way to deal with these issues of skin color.

Larsen's first novel, *Quicksand* (1928), was about a biracial woman who struggled to find her place in society. It won a Harmon Award, a money prize that recognized achievements in African-American art and literature. Her second novel, *Passing* (1929), was about two fair-skinned women—one who passed and one who didn't—and the difficulties they faced with their decisions. Larsen won the Guggenheim Fellowship for her work on this book, making her the first African-American to win this prestigious award. She used the cash prize to live in Spain for two years. While overseas, she finished her third novel, *Mirage*.

Larsen's return to the United States in 1932 was anything but joyous. Her publisher rejected the new novel. Her marriage was ending. And she lost

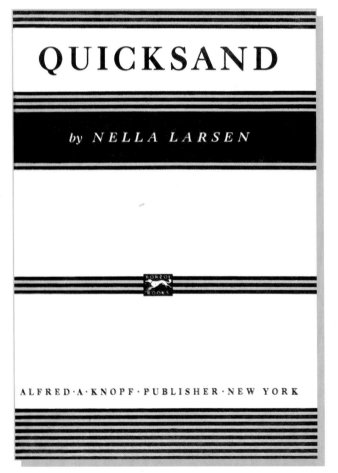

Nella Larsen's 1928 novel Quicksand *was largely autobiographical.*

many friends when she was accused of plagiarizing a story. The plagiarism, which she denied, was never proven.

These events sent her into a depression. Larsen left Harlem and never wrote again. In 1941, she returned to nursing, a career she kept until she died—alone and forgotten—in 1964.

Her rejection would end a decade later. In the 1970s, black female writers rediscovered her novels—and praised them for their honest explorations of race and the struggles of biracial women. Larsen may have died an overlooked talent, but today she is considered one of the most important writers of the Harlem Renaissance.

JESSIE FAUSET:
EDITOR AND AUTHOR

Jessie Fauset (1882–1961) was born in Camden County, New Jersey, across the Delaware River from Philadelphia, Pennsylvania. She was the daughter of a minister, and the youngest of seven children. Fauset's mother died when she was a child.

Education was important to Fauset. She was an exceptional student who graduated with honors in 1900 from the High School for Girls in Philadelphia. Dreaming of college and a career as a writer and teacher, she applied to Bryn Mawr, a women's college in Pennsylvania. But she was rejected because she was black.

Fauset refused to give up and won a scholarship to Cornell University in New York. In 1905, she became Cornell's first African-American graduate. She was also the first black woman admitted to Phi Beta Kappa, the oldest collegiate national honor society in the country. The organi-

14

zation is made up of the smartest and best students in college.

Encouraged by her success, Fauset applied to teach in the Philadelphia school district. Again she faced discrimination, but she refused to give up her dream.

In October 1906, she found work as a French and Latin teacher in Washington,

Jessie Fauset is remembered as one of the most important novelists of the Harlem Renaissance.

D.C. Over the next 13 years, she taught, wrote, and completed a master's degree in French from the University of Pennsylvania. These accomplishments were impressive for any woman at that time, regardless of race.

The heart of the campus of Cornell University in Ithaca, New York, in the 1920s

While Fauset was at Cornell, her father died. He had been her mentor, and she missed his advice. She began writing to W.E.B. DuBois for guidance and support. DuBois liked Fauset and published many of her articles in *The Crisis,* the magazine of the National

16

Association for the Advancement of Colored People (NAACP), an association dedicated to the equal treatment of African-Americans.

In 1919, DuBois hired Fauset to be literary editor of the magazine, and she moved to Harlem. One year later, he started a monthly publication for children called *The Brownies' Book* and named Fauset its editor as well.

This job, which she held until 1926, offered Fauset an inter-national stage to pro-mote her ideas about race and the importance of literature in help-ing African Americans overcome oppression.

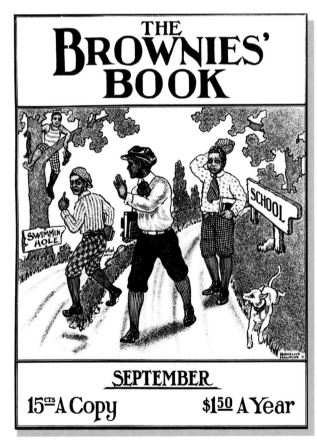

The goal of The Brownies' Book *was "to teach Universal Love and Brotherhood for all little folk—black and brown and yellow and white."*

Fauset believed that black writers ought to tell their own stories. Today, she is recognized for discovering some of the greatest authors of the Harlem Renaissance. She is often referred to as a "midwife" of the renaissance for starting so many careers. A midwife is someone who helps women give birth. Fauset helped give birth to the renaissance.

But Fauset was more than a midwife to others' careers. She wrote four novels between 1924 and 1933. Her novels were unique because they focused on how social class—or the amount of money and power one had—affected the lives of black women. Some people were critical of Fauset's emphasis on class. They thought she should focus only on race. But Fauset came from a poor family, and she knew being in a lower social class created additional barriers in American society.

In 1927, Fauset returned to teaching. She taught French in New York City schools until the early 1940s, when she and her husband, Herbert Harris, retired to

New Jersey. Fauset remained active, lecturing and hosting cultural events that promoted black writers until her death in April 1961.

Fauset is remembered as an important editor, writer, and supporter of black authors. But something else made her unique. She realized that women—not just men—could help shape the Harlem Renaissance.

The Crisis *was founded in 1910 and continues to be published today.*

ZORA NEALE HURSTON: WRITER AND ANTHROPOLOGIST

Zora Neale Hurston (1891–1960) was born in Nostasulga, Alabama, the fifth of eight children. Her parents moved the family to Eatonville, Florida, when she was a small child.

Eatonville children at play in the 1930s

Eatonville was an unusual place. It was the first town in the United States to be run completely by African-Americans. Here Hurston learned the rich history of Southern blacks and enjoyed a life free from prejudice. Eatonville was heavenly in her eyes—until tragedy struck.

Hurston was 13 years old when her mother died, a loss that deeply affected her. When her father remarried five months later, Zora decided to leave town and strike out on her own. She spent more than a decade bouncing between the homes of her older siblings all around the country. She eventually found work with a traveling theater

Author Zora Neale Hurston

company. It was during this time that she developed a love of travel and adventure.

In 1917, Hurston moved to Baltimore. The 26-year-old decided to use her youthful face to take advantage of Maryland's free schooling for black children. She told people she was 16 and headed to school. After she graduated, she enrolled in Howard University in Washington, D.C.

Howard University was established in 1867 to prepare black teachers and preachers to educate the millions of newly freed slaves.

Hurston enjoyed college and excelled at English and history. She especially liked Alain Locke's writing class. Locke was a black philosopher, educator, and writer who helped inspire not only Hurston but the entire Harlem Renaissance movement. Hurston's first story was published in the university's literary magazine in 1921. Three years later, she published an article in a national magazine.

When Hurston ran out of money for school, Locke encouraged her to move to Harlem, where she would find financial support to become a professional writer. It was not uncommon for black writers to have a wealthy white patron—someone who paid their bills—so they could write.

When she arrived in January 1925, Hurston went to parties and poetry readings and danced at jazz clubs late into the night. She loved Harlem. She once said of it: "At certain times I have no race, I am *me*."

Inspired by her new home, Hurston became the first black woman to enroll at Barnard College, a New York City liberal arts college for women. It was there that she discovered anthropology, the study of people and their cultures.

Hurston studied with Franz Boas, the leading anthropologist in the United States. Boas saw great potential in Hurston and her research. She was now a writer with a mission to travel the South and collect stories of African-American life. She set out on her adventure in 1928 and spent the next 14 years traveling and writing.

During her life, she wrote four novels, two books of folklore, an autobiography, and more than 50 essays, short stories, and plays. She also won two Guggenheim fellowships. She is perhaps best known for her

Anthropologist Franz Boas

novel *Their Eyes Were Watching God* (1937), which tells the story of a young black woman who finds freedom from gender and racial oppression.

By 1950, Hurston had returned to Florida, but her writing and her health were on the decline. To make ends

$3.00

One of the most complete collections of American negro folklore that has ever been published forms Part I. Authentic descriptions of the weird hoodoo practices as carried on by negroes in the South today composes Part II.

MULES AND MEN

By Zora Neale Hurston

Author of "Jonah's Gourd Vine"

Foreword by Dr. Franz Boas
of Columbia University

Illustrated by Covarrubias

Zora Hurston has made here probably the greatest and most sympathetically recorded collection of Negro folklore in the world (we say "folklore" but in this book B. Moseley called them "big old lies we tell when we're jus' sittin' around here on the store porch doin' nothin"). And tall lies they are about men "so black till they have to throw a sheet over their heads so de sun kin rise every mornin'." Included in the first part are folk-tales, typical sermons by colored preachers and a number of negro songs with complete musical accompaniment—the famous "John Henry," "East Coast Blues" and "Mule on De Mount." In the second section the author's equally exhaustive first-hand study of the hoodoo practices of the Southern darky is clearly evident. She explains the origin of hoodoo, describes the weird practices and rituals of the famous Marie Leveau of New Orleans, her successor and many other hoodoo doctors. No more vivid atmosphere could be created as a background for this authentic material, no more intimate facts could be told, than those which Miss Hurston brings to us here—herself a member of the richly imaginative race about which she writes.

Jacket in four colors, frontispiece and 10 black and white illustrations by Miguel Covarrubias.

In the novel Mules and Men, *Hurston wrote about Southern working-class blacks.*

25

meet, she worked as a substitute teacher and a maid. In 1959, she had a stroke and entered a nursing home in Fort Pierce, Florida, where she died on January 28, 1960. She was buried in an unmarked grave in a segregated cemetery.

Thirteen years later, writer Alice Walker revived Hurston's writing so a new generation could discover it. Walker knew that the writing was unique because it captured the stories of black Southern culture in ways no one else had before. Today, Hurston is appreciated as one of the most important writers of the 20th century.

AUGUSTA SAVAGE: SCULPTOR AND TEACHER

Augusta Savage (1892–1962) was born in Green Cove Springs, Florida, the seventh of 14 children. At an early age, Savage discovered she loved making things out of clay. But her father, a strict Methodist minister, disapproved, so she quit temporarily.

When the family moved to West Palm Beach, Florida, in 1915, she began sculpting again, thanks to

Augusta Savage with two of her sculptures in 1937

the generosity of a local potter who gave her free clay. Four years later, Savage won an award at the county fair for her sculptures. Encouraged by her success, she tried to establish herself as a portrait sculptor in Jacksonville, Florida. It was hard to find work, so in 1921, she moved to Harlem.

Savage arrived with little more than her talent and $4.60 in her pocket. She was accepted into the Cooper Union School of Art and completed the program in three years. In Harlem, she found prominent African Americans, such as W.E.B. DuBois, who were interested in having their portraits sculpted.

Savage's unique sculptures emphasized physiognomy, which refers to the portrayal of facial features—in this case, those of African-Americans. Often white artists made black subjects look ugly, but Savage showed features such as curly hair and broad noses as beautiful.

Some criticized her style, but when she faced racism in 1922, most of the Harlem community supported her. She had applied for a scholarship to study art in France, but

Since its establishment in 1859, Cooper Union has offered free education to students interested in architecture, art, and engineering.

the panel of American judges rejected her because she was black. Outraged, the African-American community notified the media. Why, Savage asked, were African-American

29

men asked to fight for democracy in France during World War I, but she was denied entrance into their schools? As a result of her public comments, white museum owners, art dealers, and critics labeled her a troublemaker—but African-Americans embraced her.

Savage refused to give up. In 1929, she won a

Julius Rosenwald Fellowship for her sculpted portrait of a young boy, titled *Gamin*. Coincidently, the award allowed her to study in Paris. Two years later, she won a second Rosenwald fellow- ship and a Carnegie Foundation grant, which allowed her

Savage may have modeled Gamin *after her young nephew, Ellis Ford.*

to continue her studies in Europe.

Savage returned to Harlem in 1932 and started the Savage Studio of Arts and Crafts, where students studied for free. An outstanding teacher, Savage was also among the most influential artists of her day. She became the first black admitted to the National Association of Women Painters and Sculptors in 1934. Three years later, she was named first director of the Harlem Community Art Center. Here she helped train a new generation of African-American artists.

One of Savage's most recognized achievements was a commission to create a sculpture for the 1939 New York World's Fair. *The Harp*, a 16-foot (4.9-meter) sculpture, was inspired by the song "Lift Every Voice and Sing." It featured 12 black figures that descended in height to form the shape of a harp. The sculpture won worldwide recognition.

Savage left Harlem in 1945 for Saugerties, New York, where she continued to sculpt and teach. Seventeen years later, her health began to fail, and she returned to New York City. She died of cancer on March 26, 1962.

Savage at work on The Harp *in her New York studio*

Known for producing great art, her greatest legacy may have been teaching a new generation of black artists. She once said of her students: "If I can inspire one of these youngsters to develop the talent I know they possess, then my monument will be in their work."

32

BESSIE SMITH: EMPRESS OF THE BLUES

Bessie Smith (1894–1937) was born in Chattanooga, Tennessee. Her parents were extremely poor and worked hard to support their family.

Life was hard for Bessie and her six siblings. Her father died when she was a baby, and her mother died when she was a young child. Bessie's oldest sister, Viola, supported the family

A contemporary painting of Bessie Smith by artist Bruni Sablan is titled The Empress.

33

by working as a laundress, while Bessie and her brother Andrew worked as street performers, singing and dancing for money. Her brother Clarence, also a performer, eventually left town with a traveling theater.

Bessie envied Clarence. She desperately wanted to leave home, too. In 1912, after finishing her freshman year at West Main Street School in Chattanooga, she joined Clarence in the theater.

Singer Gertrude "Ma" Rainey

Smith was a good dancer and an even better singer. One of the show's stars, blues singer Gertrude "Ma" Rainey, encouraged Smith to sing the blues, which has its roots in the music of Southern plantations. During the years of slavery, blacks working on plantations used songs to communicate without the slave owners' knowledge. In the late 1800s, the blues became a popular form of music among freed blacks. It flourished in certain areas of the country, including Harlem.

As a performer, Smith gained recognition for her eye-catching costumes and her outstanding voice. In 1921, she moved to Philadelphia, where she was "discovered" by Frank Walker of Columbia Records. Another singer had released a recording of a blues song titled "Crazy Blues," which became a huge hit. Other record companies wanted to make a profit from blues. Major record labels set up departments to handle what they called "race records," recordings by African-American artists. And they wanted Smith to sing for them.

In February 1923, Smith recorded her first songs, "Gulf Coast Blues" and "Down Hearted Blues." The records went on to sell about 800,000 copies, more than "Crazy Blues" had sold. Smith had arrived.

Between 1923 and 1928, Smith sold millions of records, and she often performed in Harlem. Her recordings featured the most talented black musicians of the day, including Louis Armstrong and Fletcher Henderson. While

Fletcher Henderson (seated at the piano) and Louis Armstrong (center back row) in the 1920s with members of Henderson's orchestra

traveling with her show, the *Harlem Frolics*, Smith became known as "Empress of the Blues."

After the Great Depression hit in 1929, Smith reinvented herself as a big band singer. She swept her hair back in a neat bun and wore elegant evening gowns. She embraced big band music, which involved a full orchestra with horns, drums, piano, and singer. It was sometimes called swing music because of its upbeat tempo and sound. She debuted her new style at the Apollo Theater in Harlem in the mid-1930s. Smith was back.

During Smith's big band era her dress and performances became more elegant.

37

But she would not live to enjoy her new fame for long. On September 26, 1937, Smith died in a car crash in Clarksdale, Mississippi. An estimated 7,000 people attended her funeral in Philadelphia the following week.

One historian noted that Smith "ascended to a level that no other African-American artist of her time and genre had reached." In 1970, a marker was placed on her grave that stated: "The Greatest Blues Singer in the World Will Never Stop Singing." The woman dubbed the Empress of the Blues continues to reign supreme today.

EPILOGUE: SO OTHERS MAY DREAM

In their own way, each of these extraordinary women helped shape the cultural movement that was the Harlem Renaissance. They were not content to sit by and let their

The women of the Harlem Renaissance inspired the education and work of many more generations of men and women.

fates be determined by racism and gender discrimination. They pursued education and opportunities denied to their mothers and grandmothers.

There were countless other black women who overcame such barriers. For example, Bessie Coleman became the world's first internationally licensed black pilot. The child of Texas sharecroppers, Coleman dreamt of flying. When no one in the United States would teach her, she headed to France. Seven months later, she received her license from the renowned

Bessie Coleman completed a 10-month flying course in just seven months.

Federation Aeronautique Internationale. Her dream to open an aviation school to train other black pilots was cut short in 1926 when she died in a plane accident. Three years later, however, friends opened the Bessie Coleman Aero Club in Los Angeles, California.

While Coleman never lived among the women of Harlem, their spirit inspired her—and others—to achieve their dreams.

GLOSSARY

biracial—involving members of two or more races

discrimination—treating people unfairly because of their race, religion, sex, or age

oppression—unjust acts against another person

passing—pretending to be of a different background in order to gain rights that are otherwise denied

plagiarizing—copying someone else's work and calling it your own

prejudice—hatred or unfair treatment of a group of people who belong to a certain race or religion

racism—the belief that one group of people is better than another

renaissance—a time of new ideas and artistic expression that inspires people to view the world differently

segregated—separated from others because of race

social activists—people who work to bring about positive change for all people

vaudeville—type of theater that presented long shows with many acts, including singers, comedians, and magicians

DID YOU KNOW?

- Sometimes Nella Larsen wrote using the male name Allen Semi. This is her married name, Nella Imes, spelled backward.

- Nursing was a prestigious field for young black women in the early 1900s. Most African-American women were maids, nannies, laundresses, or waitresses.

- Jessie Fauset used *The Crisis* to promote Pan-Africanism, the belief that black people around the world should unite in the struggle for freedom.

- In the early 1900s, many African-Americans were denied entrance to college. In 1917 there were only 2,132 African-American college students nationwide. In 2002, the U.S. Department of Education counted more than 1.9 million African-American college students.

- Zora Neale Hurston carried a pistol for protection on her travels to the South. Very few people—especially women—traveled alone in the 1920s and 1930s. It was considered very dangerous.

IMPORTANT DATES

Timeline

1909	The National Association for the Advancement of Colored People (NAACP) is formed.
1918	The Great Northern Migration reaches its height, as black sharecroppers seek better opportunities in Northern cities.
1919	The "Harlem Hellfighters"—a unit of black World War I soldiers—return to Harlem in a glorious parade.
1920	Women gain the right to vote; however, black women are still denied equal rights at the polls.
1925	Alain Locke publishes *The New Negro*, the book that helps shape the Harlem Renaissance.
1929	The Great Depression impacts the arts in Harlem because people can no longer afford to go to the theater, buy books, or go listen to jazz as they did before.

IMPORTANT PEOPLE

JOSEPHINE BAKER (1906–1975)
Dancer who went to Paris in 1925 and gained international fame

GWENDOLYN BENNETT (1902–1981)
Writer, painter, and poet who was considered one of the most versatile of Harlem's writers and artists

MARITA ODETTE BONNER (1898–1971)
Once the forgotten writer of the Harlem Renaissance but now recognized as sharing equal importance with Nella Larsen, Jessie Fauset, and Zora Neale Hurston for her contributions to the literary arts

A'LELIA WALKER (1885–1931)
Businesswoman and socialite who held memorable teas for Harlem poets, writers, and sculptors at her townhouse known as the "Dark Tower"

DOROTHY WEST (1907–1998)
Novelist, short-story writer, and editor who founded a literary magazine called Challenge, *which sought to revitalize the fading impact of the Harlem Renaissance after the Great Depression*

WANT TO KNOW MORE?

At the Library

Chambers, Veronica. *The Harlem Renaissance.* Broomall, Pa.: Chelsea
    House Publishers, 1997.

Haskins, James. *Black Stars of the Harlem Renaissance.* New York: Wiley, 2002.

Jacques, Geoffrey. *Free Within Ourselves: The Harlem Renaissance.* New York:
    Franklin Watts, 1996.

Jordan, Denise. *Harlem Renaissance Artists.* Chicago: Heinemann Library, 2003.

Manera, Alexandria. *Bessie Smith.* Chicago: Raintree, 2003.

McKissack, Patricia, and Fredrick McKissack. *Zora Neale Hurston, Writer
    and Storyteller*. Berkeley Heights, N.J.: Enslow, 2002.

On the Web

For more information on this topic, use FactHound.

1. Go to *www.facthound.com*

2. Type in this book ID: 0756520347

3. Click on the *Fetch It* button.

FactHound will find the best Web sites for you.

On the Road

**The Zora Neale Hurston National
Museum of Fine Arts**
227 E. Kennedy Blvd.
Eatonville, FL 32751
407/647-3307
Displays of work by artists of
African descent

**The National Afro-American
Museum and Cultural Center**
1350 Brush Row Road
Wilberforce, Ohio 45382
Displays of photographs, artifacts,
and artwork that celebrate the history of African-Americans; includes
sculptures by Augusta Savage

Look for more We the People books about this era:

The American Newsboy
Angel Island
The Great Chicago Fire
Great Women of the Suffrage Movement
The Harlem Renaissance
The Haymarket Square Tragedy
The Hindenburg

Industrial America
The Johnstown Flood
The Lowell Mill Girls
The Orphan Trains
Roosevelt's Rough Riders
Yellow Journalism

A complete list of We the People titles is available on our Web site:
www.compasspointbooks.com

INDEX

About the Author

Lisa Beringer McKissack writes nonfiction books for children and is a part-time college instructor of sociology and women's studies. She has a master's degree in American Studies from Penn State University-Harrisburg. She lives in Fort Wayne, Indiana, with her husband, Fred McKissack Jr., and her son, Mark. In her free time, she loves to read and grow vegetables in her garden.